LI

LOVE

DIMENSIONS

FOR LIVING

NASHVILLE

To my darling daughter Suzanne.

Love always,
Mama.
Feb. 1999

INTRODUCTION

John, one of Jesus Christ's twelve disciples, has been called 'the apostle of love'. John's gospel is full of Jesus' teaching about Christian love: 'God so loved the world ... love one another ... the greatest love a person can have for his friends is to give his life for them.'

John's first letter continues this theme: 'God is love ... love comes from God ... This is what love is: it is not that we loved God, but that he loved us and sent his Son ...'

There is a story about John as a very old man, after he had written the Book of Revelation exiled on the island of Patmos. He was too weak to walk, so he was carried into a room of Christians. They all longed for him to preach, but he only had the strength to repeat these words three times: 'Little children, love one another.'

Saints, divines, writers, poets and statesmen, from the first century to the twentieth century, share their thoughts on Christian love in this book. It is designed to be a blessing and comfort to all who read it; for as part of the quotation from Dostoevsky puts it, 'Love will teach us all things'.

LOVE IS SWIFT

Love is swift, sincere, pious, pleasant, faithful, prudent, longsuffering, strong and never seeking her own; for wherever you seek your own, you fall from love.

Thomas à Kempis, The Imitation of Christ

THE REASON
FOR LOVING

The reason for loving God
is God himself and
how he should be loved
is to love without limit.

Bernard of Clairvaux,
On Loving God

LEARNING LOVE

They who learn love,
will always be its scholars.

Byron, Don Juan

KINDNESS

Kindness is a language which the
blind can see and the deaf can hear.

Author unknown

THE HEART OF JESUS

You will find all that is lacking in your heart in the heart of Jesus, dying on the cross. Then you will be enabled to love those whom you would naturally, in your pride, hate and crush.

Archbishop François Fenelon,
Christian Perfection

I am the rose of Sharon, and the lily of the valleys. As the lily among thorns, so is my love among the daughters.

Song of Solomon 2:1,2

THE GREATEST IS LOVE

I may have all the faith needed
to move mountains -
but if I have no love, I am nothing.
I may give away everything I have,
and even give my body to be burnt -
but if I have no love,
this does me no good.
Love is patient and kind.

Love never gives up.
Love is eternal.
Faith, hope and love remain;
and the greatest of these is love.

The apostle Paul, The Bible,
1 Corinthians 13

BE LOVABLE

If you be loved,
love and be lovable.

Benjamin Franklin,
Poor Richard's Almanac, 1755

THE ROOT AND THE FRUIT

Love of God is the root, love of our
neighbor the fruit of the Tree of Life.
Neither can exist without the other, but the
one is cause and the other effect.

Archbishop William Temple,
Readings on St John's Gospel

ONE MUST LOVE ALWAYS

Love will teach us all things: but we must learn how to win love; it is got with difficulty: it is a possession dearly bought with much labour and in long time; for one must love not sometimes only, for a passing moment, but always. There is no man who does not sometimes love: even the wicked can do that.

Fyodor Dostoevsky, The Brothers Karamozov

JESUS' COMMAND
ABOUT LOVE

Love the Lord your God
with all your heart,
with all your soul,
and with all your mind.

Jesus Christ, the Bible,
Matthew 22:37

AN INSTANT OF PURE LOVE

An instant of pure love is more
precious to God and the soul, and
more profitable to the church,
than all other good works together,
though it may seem as if nothing
were done.

St John of the Cross

FILLED WITH LOVE

He who is filled with love is filled
with God himself.

Augustine of Hippo

THE FOUNDATION OF LOVE

Alexander, Caesar, Charlemagne and I founded empires; but upon what did we rest the creations of our genius? Upon force. Jesus Christ alone founded his empire upon love; and at this hour millions of men would die for him.

Napoleon

THE BEGINNING OF LOVE

Let us make God the beginning and end of
our love, for he is the fountain from which
all things flow and into him alone they
flow back. Let him therefore be the
beginning of our love.

Richard Rolle

BATHED IN THE ESSENCE OF GOD

When through love the soul goes beyond all the images in the mind, and is taken out of itself it flows into God: then is God its peace and fullness.

It loses itself in the Godhead; but so to lose itself is rather to find itself. This soul is, as it were, all God-colored, because its essence is bathed in the Essence of God.

Louis of Blois, Benedictine Abbot, died 1566

THE MORE WE LOVE

The more we love, the better we are,
and the greater our friendships are,
the dearer we are to God.

Jeremy Taylor

IT'S NEVER TOO LATE TO LOVE GOD

Late have I loved Thee, O Beauty so ancient and so new; late have I loved Thee! Thou didst breathe fragrance upon me, and I drew in my breath and do now pant for Thee: I tasted Thee, and now hunger and thirst for Thee: Thou didst touch me, and I have burned for Thy peace.

St Augustine 'Confessions'

PURE LOVE

Pure love comes to God himself,
to abide in him,
but not to seek anything
from him.

St Thomas Aquinas

LOVE THY NEIGHBOR

There are only two duties which our Lord requires of us, namely, the love of God, and the love of our neighbor. In my opinion, the surest sign for discovery whether we observe these two duties, is the love of our neighbor. And be assured that the more you advance in the love of your neighbor, the more you advance in the love of God.

St Teresa of Avila

THE EXTENT OF LOVE

You are as prone to love as the sun is to shine, it being the most delightful and natural employment of the soul of man, without which you are dark and miserable. Consider therefore the extent of love, its vigour and excellency. For certainly he that delights not in love makes vain the universe, and is of necessity to himself the greatest burden.

Thomas Traherne

LOVE FOR THE
WHOLE HUMAN RACE

Because our Savior has shown in the parable of the good Samaritan (Luke 10:36) that the term 'neighbor' includes the most distant stranger, there is no excuse for limiting the maxim of love to our own circle. God demands that the love we bear to him should be spread abroad among all mankind. Our basic principle must always be that whatever a person may be like, we must still love him, because we love God.

Brother Lawrence

If instead of a gem, or even a flower, we should cast the gift of a loving thought into the heart of a friend, that would be giving as the angels give.

George Macdonald

LOVE YOUR NEIGHBOR TODAY

TODAY – Mend a quarrel. Search out a forgotten friend. Dismiss suspicion and replace it with trust. Write a love letter. Share some treasure. Give a soft answer. Encourage youth. Manifest your loyalty in a word or a deed.

Author unknown

TODAY

TODAY – Keep a promise. Find the time.
Forego a grudge. Forgive an enemy.
Listen. Apologize if you were wrong. Try
to understand. Flout envy. Examine your
demands on others. Think first of
someone else. Appreciate, be kind, be
gentle. Laugh a little more.

Author unknown

Our attitude to all men would be Christian if we regarded them as though they were dying, and determined our relation to them in the light of death, both their death and of our own. A person who is dying calls forth a special kind of feeling. Our attitude to him is at once softened and lifted on to a higher plane. We then can feel compassion for people whom we did not love. But every man is dying, I too am dying and must never forget about death.

N. Berdyaev

Jesu, Lover of my soul,
Let me to thy bosom fly,
While the nearer waters roll,
While the tempest still is high:
Hide me, O my Savior, hide,
Till the storm of life be past!
Safe into the haven guide,
Oh, receive my soul at last!
Other refuge have I none,
Hangs my helpless soul on thee;
Leave, ah! leave me not alone,
Still support and comfort me:
All my trust on thee is stayed,
All my help from thee I bring;
Cover my defenseless head
With the shadow of thy wing.

Charles Wesley

It is love alone that counts,
love alone that triumphs,
and love alone that endures.

Karl Barth

Don't waste time bothering about whether you love your neighbor; act as if you did. As soon as we do this we discover one of the great secrets. When you are behaving as if you love someone, you will presently come to love him. If you injure someone you dislike, you will find yourself disliking him more. If you do him a good turn, you will find yourself disliking him less.

C.S. Lewis, Mere Christianity

Love is a fruit in season at all times, and within reach of every hand. Anyone may gather it and no limit is set. Everyone can reach this love through meditation, spirit of prayer and sacrifice, by an intense inner life.

Mother Teresa of Calcutta

THE NEED FOR LOVE

The biggest disease today is not leprosy or tuberculosis, but rather the feeling of being unwanted, uncared for, and deserted by everybody.

Mother Teresa of Calcutta

GOD SO LOVED...

For God so loved the world that he gave his one and only Son, that whoever believes in him shall not perish but have eternal life.

The Bible, John chapter 3, verse 16

LITTLE THINGS OUT OF LOVE

We should, once and for all, entrust ourselves to God, abandon ourselves to him alone. We must not grow weary in doing little things for the love of God, who looks not on the greatness of the deed, but to the love of the deed.

Brother Lawrence

Daughter, if you knew how sweet
your love is to me, you would
never do anything else but love
me with all your heart.

Catherine of Siena

All things are possible to him
who believes, yet more to him
who hopes, more still to him
who loves, and most of all to
him who practices and
perseveres in these
three virtues.

Brother Lawrence

It is our care for the helpless, our practice of lovingkindness, that brands us in the eyes of many of our opponents. 'Look!' they say. 'How they love one another! Look, they are prepared to die for one another.'

Tertullian

God's love is like
the River Amazon flowing
down to water one daisy.

Anonymous

CONTEMPLATION

Contemplation is nothing else but a secret,
peaceful, and loving infusion of God,
which if admitted, will set the soul on fire
with the spirit of love.

St John of the Cross

Three stages of growth in maturity
Love of self for self's sake;
Love of God for self's sake;
Love of God for God.

St Bernard of Clairvaux

LOVE IS...

Love is the abridgement
of all theology.

St Francis de Sales

Charity is the great channel through which God passes all his mercy upon mankind. For we receive forgiveness of our sins in proportion to our forgiving our brother. Certain it is, that God cannot, will not, never did, reject a charitable man in his greatest needs and in his passionate prayers; for God himself is love, and every degree of charity that dwells in us is the participation of the divine nature.

Jeremy Taylor

ONE LOVING ACT

If I can stop one heart from breaking,
I shall not live in vain;
If I can ease one life the aching,
Or cool one pain,
Or help one fainting robin
Unto his nest again,
I shall not live in vain.

Emily Dickinson